This Water
ये जो जल

Gagan Gill

This Water
ये जो जल

Translated from Hindi by
Lucy Rosenstein with Jane Duran

poetry
translation
centre

First published in 2020
by the Poetry Translation Centre Ltd
The Albany, Douglas Way, London, SE8 4AG

www.poetrytranslation.org

Poems © Gagan Gill 2020
English Translations © Lucy Rosenstein and Jane Duran 2020
Introduction © Lucy Rosenstein 2020
Afterword © Helen Charman 2020
Jane Duran Photograph © Caroline Forbes

Some of these poems first appeared in *Poetry Review* and *Soundings* and the chapbook *Poems* (Enitharmon; 2008).

ISBN: 978-1-9161141-5-9

A catalogue record for this book is available from the British Library

Typeset in Minion / Arial Unicode by Poetry Translation Centre Ltd

Series Editor: Edward Doegar
Cover Design: Kit Humphrey
Printed in the UK by TJ Books Limited

The PTC is supported using public funding by
Arts Council England

Contents

Introduction	7
A Desire in the Bangles	11
Child, Go Home	15
Fish	17
Ants	19
Every Love	21
You Will Turn in Your Sleep	23
Only for a Day	27
You Will Say Night	31
Someone is Placing Tracks	35
Do You See It?	41
Sometimes in Your Clouds	47
This Water	51

Afterword	57
About the contributors	64
About the series	66

Introduction

Gagan Gill was born in Delhi in 1959. Her studies in English literature, journalism and film led her to a distinguished career as a journalist and a translator. For eleven years she was the literary editor of the *Times of India* magazine *Vama* and the *Sunday Observer*. She edited a book on the famous Indian artist Ram Kumar and a special issue on women's writing in Hindi for the English literary magazine *Yathra*. During this period, she published ten volumes of translations including work by Zbigniew Herbert, Harbhajan Singh, Sitakant Mahapatra and Shrikant Verma. After her extremely successful career as a literary editor, she chose to withdraw from the world of journalism in order to secure the 'long periods of silence in her everyday life' which she considered necessary to remain 'truly connected to words'.

Gill has published five books of poetry and four volumes of prose. Even though it was her poetry which first attracted the attention of readers and critics, and which is celebrated in this volume, over the years her prose has become an equally important part of her oeuvre. *Awaak* (*Speechless*), her account of her pilgrimage of the Mount Kailash near Mansarovar lake is widely acknowledged as a ground-breaking piece of prose; it is included in BBC's survey of best travelogues written in Hindi.

Gill's achievements are even more astounding set against the background of a literary canon where women's voices are rarely heard. Her only antecedents recognised by the Hindi literary establishment as major poets are Mira and Mahadevi Verma. She differs from her predecessors in that, although she is firmly rooted in the Indian cultural tradition – for example, the Buddha's four noble truths are reflected in much of her writing – she is also a writer of 'exceptionally cosmopolitan poetic sensibility' (Trivedi). This is reflected by her recognition outside India: she was invited by the International Writing Program in Iowa in 1990, the Nieman Fellowship for Journalism at Harvard University in 1992-93, the Goethe Institute in 2000 and the Poetry Translation Centre in 2005. Her works are taught in several American, English and German universities.

One could write a lengthy list of Gagan Gill's achievements: the languages into which her books have been translated, the prestigious literary prizes she has been awarded. But this is not the reason why her poems should be translated into English. The imperative to make her verses accessible to the English-speaking reader stems from their intensity and poignancy. She writes about pain without any sentimentality or gushiness. Her poems are understated, deceptively simple, occasionally prosaic, full of repetitions and yet exquisitely crafted. She combines stark images with rare expressiveness: expressiveness composed of silences, gaps, absences, disruptions, of pulsational pressure which goes beyond language.

Lucy Rosenstein

Poems

एक इच्छा चूड़ियों में

एक इच्छा लड़की की चूड़ियों में चलती है
पहले वह टूटें उसके बिस्तर पर
फिर टूटें उसकी चौखट पर

लेकिन चौखट पर क्यों?

क्योंकि लड़की के भीतर एक शोकमथी औरत है
औरत जो विधवा है
है नहीं लेकिन
हो जाएगी जो

लड़की का डर उसकी धमनियों से काँपता
चूड़ियों तक चलता है
काँपती है उनमें लड़की की इच्छा
काँपती है उनमें लड़की का शोक

शोक?

आदमी कहाँ है लड़की का?
आदमी जिसका मातम उसकी धमनियों में है
और इच्छा जिसकी उसकी चूड़ियों में

आदमी उसका फँसा है
किसी दूसरी देह में
किसी दूसरे सपने में,
दूसरे दुख, दूसरे आँसू में
उसका हर दुख, सपना, आँसू
लड़की की मातमी पकड़ से परे है...

A Desire in the Bangles

A desire is in the girl's bangles:
first they will break on his bed
then on the threshold of his house.

But why on the threshold?

Because in the girl there is a woman
mourning – who is not yet
a widow
but a widow to be.

The girl's fear throbs in her veins
as far as her bangles
The girl's desire throbs in them
The girl's mourning throbs in them

Mourning?

Where is the girl's man
for whom mourning runs in her veins
for whom desire is in her bangles?

Her man is caught
in some other body
some other dream
sorrow, other tears
His every sorrow, dream, tear
is beyond the reach of the mourning girl . . .

लेकिन लड़की तो लड़की है
उसमें वही आदिम भोलापन
पागलपन, मरनपन भरा है
जिसकी सजा
किसी आनेवाले कल
वह उस आदमी को देगी

जब तोड़ेगी अपनी चूड़ियाँ...

But the girl is only a girl –
in her is that primal innocence,
madness, death,
whose punishment
she will give to that man
one day

when she will break her bangles . . .

बच्चे, तुम अपने घर जाओ

बच्चे, तुम अपने घर जाओ

घर कहीं नहीं है?
तो वापस कोख में जाओ

माँ की कोख नहीं है?
पिता के वीर्य में जाओ

पिता कहीं नहीं है?
तो माँ के गर्भ में जाओ

गर्भ का अंडा बंजर?
तो मुन्ना झर जाओ तुम
उसकी माहवारी में

जाती है जैसे उसकी
इच्छा संडास के नीचे
वैसे तुम भी जाओ

लड़की को मुक्त करो अब
बच्चे, तुम अपने घर जाओ

Child, Go Home

Child, go home.

Your home is nowhere?
Then go back to the womb.

No mother's womb?
Go to father's semen.

Your father is nowhere?
Go to mum's tubes.

Is the egg there barren?
Then, little one, flow away
in her menstrual blood

just as her longing
goes down the drain –
go that way too.

Let the girl be.
Child, go home.

मछली

इस मछली के मस्तिष्क में
जल नहीं
आकाश भर गया है

पानी नहीं
उड़ने की लालसा
भर गयी है
इस मछली की देह में

भरे समुद्र में वह
खाली कर रही है स्वयं को
अनवरत सदियों से

छोटी-बड़ी मछलियों के
बीच से गुज़रती
चिंतन-मग्ना यह मछली
पूछती है खुद से –
समुद्र कहाँ गया
तुम्हारा ओ?

तैरती हुई मछली
दोहराती है यह प्रश्न
जैसे प्रार्थना-मंत्र हो
जानती नहीं मछली
आकाश भर गया है
उसके मस्तिष्क में

कि कपाल-क्रिया उसकी
शुरू हो चुकी है
भीतर से

Fish

No water
only sky
fills this fish's brain.

No water
but a longing to fly
is in this fish's body.

Into the brimming ocean
she is emptying herself
incessantly, over centuries.

She passes by
small fish, big fish.
Lost in thought, this fish
asks herself *oh,*
where did your ocean
go?

The swimming fish
repeats this question
as if it were a prayer-mantra.
The fish does not know
that sky has filled
her brain

that the skull-smashing ritual
has already begun
inside her.

चींटियाँ

चींटियाँ अपने घर का रास्ता भूल गयी थीं।

हमारी नींद और हमारी देह के बीच वे कतार बनातीं चलतीं। उनकी स्मृति में बिखरा रहता उनका अदृश्य आटा, जो किसी दूसरे देश-काल ने बिखेरा था। उसे ढूँढती वह चलती जातीं पृथ्वी के एक सिरे से दूसरे की ओर। वे अपने दांत गड़ातीं हर जीवित व मृत वस्तु में। उनके चलने से पृथ्वी के दुख इतने हल्के होने लगते कि दिशाएं घूमने लगतीं, भ्रमित हो। ध्रुव बदलने लगते अपनी जगह। चींटियों का दुख लेकिन कोई न जानता था।

बहुत पहले शायद कभी वे स्त्रियाँ रही हों।

Ants

The ants had lost their way home.

They walked, making lines between our sleep and our bodies. Their invisible flour stays scattered in their memory, scattered by some other place and time. They kept going from one end of the earth to the other in search of it. They sank their teeth in every living and dead thing. The sorrows of the earth grew so light with their journeying that directions began to spin in confusion. The poles began to change places. But nobody knew the ants' sorrow.

Long ago, perhaps they were women.

हर प्रेम

हर प्रेम सबसे पहले यही पूछता है, तुम्हारी चौखट तक आकर – क्या तुम मेरे लिए कूद सकते हो खिड़की से नीचे? कर सकते हो क्या तुम छलनी अपना सीना? हर प्रेम पूछता है यही, उड़ सकते हो क्या मेरे साथ, ठूँठ अपने कंधों से?

प्रेम जब आता है तुम्हारी चौखट तक, तो जल्दी चले जाने के लिए नहीं। उसे जाना होता है किसी पर्वत या घाटी की तरफ। समुद्र या नदी की तरफ। वह बिना किसी पूर्व-योजना के आ निकलता है तुम्हारे घर की तरफ, और जानना चाहता है, तुम उसके साथ डूबने चल रहे या नहीं।

प्रेम तुम्हें भली-भाँति मरने की पूरी मोहलत देता है।

Every Love

When it arrives on your doorstep, the first thing every love asks is: can you jump from the window for me? Can you stab your heart for me? Every love asks this: can you fly with me, with only the stumps of your arms?

When love arrives on your doorstep, it will not leave soon. It has to go to some mountain or valley. To an ocean or river. It comes to your house out of the blue, and wants to know if you will come along to drown with it or not.

Every love gives you enough time to die for it.

करवट बदलोगे तुम नींद में

पलकें झर जायेंगी
तुम्हें देखने की इच्छा में

उँगलियाँ बन जायेंगी
चींटियाँ
तुम्हारे पैरों पर
चढ़तीं
बिछलतीं

होंठ बन जायेंगे
नन्हीं मक्खी, नन्हा मच्छर
रखते तुम्हारे कानों पर
अपना पहला स्पर्श

साँस उसकी
करेगी चहल-कदमी
तुम्हारी सोयी काया में
यों बेखटके
जैसे खाली घर में हो

करवट बदलोगे तुम
नींद में
और तुम्हें कुछ
मालूम न होगा
    न यह
    कि क्यों भटकते रहते हैं
    कुछ प्रेम
    इस धरती पर

You Will Turn in Your Sleep

Eyelashes will fall
in her desire to see you

fingers will become
ants
crawling
slipping
on your feet

lips will be
a tiny fly, a tiny mosquito
placing on your ears
their first touch

her breath
will wander
in your sleeping body
mindlessly
as if in an empty house

you will turn
in your sleep
and you will not know
anything
>   neither
>   why some loves
>   roam restlessly
>   on this earth

न यह
कि व्यस्त रहते हैं क्यों
कीट-पतंगे
दिन-रात

तीसरे पहर तुम
उठ बैठोगे
कुछ नींद
कुछ प्यास
कुछ चित्त-भ्रम में

काफी देर
तुम्हें मालूम न होगा

क्यों हिल रही है
सारी सृष्टि
इस पहर

सुबक रहा है कौन
कहाँ?
भीतर
कि बाहर?

    यह आकांक्षा समय नहीं

      nor
      why
      insects are busy
      day and night

In the small hours
you will wake and sit up
a little sleepy
a little thirsty
a little confused

for a while
you won't know

why all creation
is shaking
in these hours

who is crying quietly
and where?
Inside
or outside?

      This is not the hour of desire.

सिर्फ़ एक दिन

सिर्फ़ एक दिन
वह नहीं सोचेगी
तुम्हारे बारे में

और मछलियाँ भूल जायेंगी
जल के भीतर अपना रास्ता

टँगा रह जायेगा जलता सूर्य
निरुपाय सौरमंडल में

फँस जायेगी समय की नाल
गिर्द अपने ही कंठ के

सिर्फ़ एक दिन
वह स्मृतिहीना
रखेगी अपना दिया
सूर्य और चंद्र के बीच

और चिंतित हो जायेंगे
आकाश में सप्त-ऋषि

झरने लगेंगे अक्षर
टूट कर लिपियों से
भूल जायेंगे जीव अपने मुख
और दर्पण कहीं न होंगे

सिर्फ़ एक दिन
क्षण भर को उससे

Only for a Day

Only for a day
she will not think
about you

and fish will lose
their way in the water

the burning sun will hang
helpless in its orbit

the umbilical cord of time
will wind round its own neck

Only for a day
she, forgetful,
will place her lamp
between the sun and moon

and the seven sages
of the heavens will be anxious

letters will shatter
after breaking away from scripts

souls will forget their faces
and there will be no mirrors

Only for a day
you will vanish

ओझल होगे तुम
दैवी कुहेलिका में

और छा जायेगा अंधकार
ब्रह्मांड के अंत तक
घुमड़ने लगेंगे लावे
पृथ्वी के अंतर में

घोंघे जल उठेंगे
अपने खोल के भीतर
कई मीलों तक

सिर्फ़ एक दिन के
विस्-मरण में
नीली पड़ जायेगी यह देह

अपने ही काटे से

in an ethereal mist,
a moment

and darkness will spread
to the ends of the universe
lava will gather
inside the earth

and cockles burn
in their shells
for miles

Only for a day's
oblivion
this body will turn blue

with its own bite

तुम कहोगे, रात

तुम कहोगे, रात
और रात हो जायेगी

तुम कहोगे, दिन
और धुल जायेगा दिन

तुम कहोगे, रंग
और उड़ती चली आयेंगी
तितलियाँ पृथ्वी-भर की

तुम सोचोगे, प्रेम
और दिगंत खोल देगा
एक इन्द्र-धनुष गुप्त

तुम होगे, संतप्त
और जल जायेगी
उसकी त्वचा
दूसरे शहर में

    तुम कहोगे, रात
    और झरती चली जायेगी स्मृति
    तुम कहोगे, दिन
    और रिक्त हो जायेगी पृथ्वी

तुम रहोगे, चुप
और चटक जायेंगी
शिलाएं चंद्रमा तक

You Will Say Night

You will say night
and night will be

You will say day
and day will be washed

You will say colour
and all the butterflies
of the earth will come flying

You will think love
and the horizon will open
a hidden rainbow

You will be tormented
and in another city
her skin
will burn

> *You will say night*
> *and memory will fall away*
> *You will say day*
> *and the earth will be empty*

You will be silent
and rocks will explode
as far away as the moon

तुम करोगे, अदेखा
और वह जा फँसेगी
अदृश्या
हवा के कंठ में

तुम कहोगे, रात
और बनने लगेगा
आप-ही-आप
रेत में एक घर

तुम कहोगे, दिन
और उघड़ जायेगी यह देह
जरा की कुतरी हुई

You will not look at her
and she will be caught
invisible
in the throat of the wind

You will say night
and a house
will rise
in the sand

You will say day
and this body, gnawed by old age
will be naked

कोई रख रहा है पटरियाँ

कोई बना रहा है तुम्हारी प्रतिमा
खींच रहा है रेखाएं
पीड़ा की
तुम्हारे मांस में

थपथपा रहा है
गीली मिट्टी
तुम्हारे चेहरे पर

पटरियां ये अदृश्य
इन्हीं पर चलना है
जीवन भर तुम्हें

मत करो गीला
इस मिट्टी को
रोज़ रोज़ लौटते
किसी बादल से

कोई उकेर रहा है तुम्हारी हड्डी
लिख रहा है अपनी लिपि
तुम्हारे माथे पर

दर्ज कर रहा है
तुम्हारा खाता
सफेद स्याह

बार-बार उछलो मत
वेदन से

Someone is Placing Tracks

Someone is sculpting your head
drawing lines
of suffering
in your flesh

patting
the wet clay
of your face

These invisible tracks
you will walk on
all your life

Don't dampen
this clay
day after day
with some cloud

Someone is carving into your bones
writing his script
on your forehead

recording
your accounts
in black and white

Don't jump up again and again
in pain

हथौड़ी लग गयी जो
उसकी उंगली पर?

सुखा रहा है
तुम्हारी मिट्टी कोई
अंदर से बाहर तक
धूप में
छाया में

सिर्फ उसी को पता है
कितनी गर्म होनी चाहिए
तुम्हारी भट्टी

कितना वह तपाये तुम्हें
कितने समय तक
कि बर्तन से तुम्हारे फिर
न भाप रिसे
न जल

एक दिन
वह लिपि
निकलेगी
राख में से बाहर

अनजान कोई हाथ
समेटेगा तुम्हारी अस्थियां
देखेगा
वह लिखावट

What if the hammer hits
his finger?

Someone is drying
your clay
from the inside out
in sun
in shade

Only he knows
how hot
your kiln should be

how long
he should bake you
so this pot of yours
will not leak steam
or water

One day
his script
will emerge
from the ashes

Some unknown hands
will gather your bones
and see
this scribble

मछलियां कुतरेंगी तुम्हें
सूरज चमकेगा
जल के ऊपर

अभी तुम
न ऊपर
न नीचे

सिहरो मत

करने दो उसे
अपना काम

देखने दो
मूरत कोई
अब भी
बनी कि नहीं

गुज़र जाने दो
मुख पर से अपने
काल का घोड़ा

हिलो मत

कोई रख रहा है
रेल की पटरियाँ
तुम्हारे चेहरे पर

Fish will gnaw at you
the sun will shine
on water

For now you are
neither above
nor below

Don't cringe

Let him finish
his job

Let him see
if the image
is finished yet
or not

Let the hoof of time
step on your face

Don't move

Someone is placing
rail lines
on your face

दिख जाता है तुम्हें

दिख जाता है तुम्हें
वहाँ आकाश से
हमारा लाल दिल?

पत्ती का हरा
कीड़े का मटमैला दिल?

दिख जाता है
वहाँ ऊपर से
कहाँ छिपा है कांटा?

कहाँ कपट
कहाँ प्रार्थना?

सुन लेते हो
सही-सही
हर वर्ण
हर ध्वनि?

पहचान लेते हो अलग
पीड़ा को क्षोभ से?

और वह
जो कुछ भी नहीं
कह पाता तुमसे
प्रार्थना में
मौन उसका दारुण
सुन पाते हो
कि नहीं?

Do You See It?

From up there
do you see
our red heart

the green of a leaf
the muddy heart of a worm?

From up there
can you see
where the thorn is hiding

where deceit
where prayer?

Can you hear
well enough
every grumble
every tone?

Can you tell suffering
from despair?

And if there is one
who says nothing
in his prayer
do you hear
his silent anguish?

भूल तो नहीं जाते
किसने पुकारा था तुम्हें
पहले
किसने बाद में?

पड़ा रहता है नास्तिक जो
मुरझाया सा धूप में
उसे भी छूते हो न
अपनी करुणा से?

याद तो रहता है न
कब होना है तुम्हें सहस्र रूप?
कब एक रूप?

कब खेलना है
बच्चों से
कब गायों से?

कब कर देना है उन्मत्त
किसी राजकुमारी को
प्रेम से अपने
फिर चखाना है उसे
रास्तों की धूल?

नचाना है फकीर को कब
था-था थैया

कौन-सी कठपुतली का
खींचना है
धागा कब
याद तो रहता है सब?

Do you ever forget
who called out to you
first
who later?

The sceptic lying shrivelled
in the sunshine
do you touch him too
with your mercy?

You remember, don't you
when to take a thousand forms
when just one?

When to play
with children
and when with cows?

When to make a princess
go mad with your love
then make her taste
the dust of the roads?

When to make a fakir dance
thaa-thaa-thaiyaa

Which puppet's string
to pull
and when
Do you remember all that?

कब पकड़ लेना है
किस के रथ का चक्का

कर देना है कब समय ऐसा
कि न वह दिन हो, न रात
न धरती, न आकाश
न काल, न अकाल

कब उड़ा देना है किसको
फूँक से
हवा में

सध तो जाता है न
तुमसे सब?

इतनी गड़बड़ ये दुनिया

झोल तो नहीं
पड़ जाता
तुम्हारे तराजू में

कभी-कभी ईश्वर?

When to seize
the wheel of whose chariot

When to play a trick
so it is neither day nor night
neither earth nor sky
neither Time nor beyond

Who to send flying off
on a puff of air
and when

You make all this
happen, don't you?

This world is so messy

Do the ropes holding
your two scales
ever get tangled

my Lord?

तुम्हारे बादल में कभी

तुम्हारे बादल में कभी
तुम्हारी बिजली में कभी
उड़ती जाती उसकी
नन्हीं सी जान

देखो प्रभु
इसका हौसला

न पानी का खौफ
न अंधेरे की चिंता

न तिनके की चाह
न साथ की परवाह

देखो प्रभु
इसका पंख
कैसा भीगा हुआ
उड़ता

ज़रूर इसे मालूम था
जाल के बारे में
जाल के ऊपर
आकाश के बारे में

ज़रूर इसे मालूम है
बादल के पीछे
सूरज के बारे में

Sometimes in Your Clouds

Sometimes in your clouds
sometimes in your lightning
a tiny life
keeps flying

Oh Lord
look at her spirit

neither fear of water
nor dread of the dark

no wish for a blade of grass
or a mate

Oh Lord
look at her feathers
so drenched
yet flying

Of course she knew
about the nets
and the sky
above them

of course she knows
about the sun
behind the clouds

घुमड़ता ज़रूर था
कोई तूफ़ान इसके सीने में

आ नहीं जाता यूँ ही कोई
बाहर के अंधड़ में

उधर आकाश में नहीं
इधर देखो प्रभु
इस मुनिया के सीने में

छोटा-सा तूफ़ान एक
उड़ता हुआ

A storm must have gathered
in her ribcage

who else would fly out just like that
into a violent dust storm?

Not over there in the sky
look here, Lord
In the breast of this songbird

a tiny storm
gathering

ये जो जल

ये जो जल
मैं पीती हूँ
हवा जो खाती हूँ
धूप जो सेंकती हूँ

न ये जल है
न हवा
न धूप

ये जो रंग मैं देखती हूँ
फूल में
लाल पर सफेद
पंखुड़ी में घूमता

कभी वृत्त
कभी रेखा में

न ये लाल है
न सफेद

न फूल
न पंखुड़ी

न वृत्त
न रेखा

ये जो
खेलते हो तुम
इस दिल से

This Water

This water
I drink
air I breathe
sunlight I bask in

is neither water
nor air
nor sunlight

This colour I see
in the flower
white on red
whirling in the petal

at times a circle
at times a line

is neither red
nor white

neither flower
nor petal

neither circle
nor line

The games
you play
with this heart

कभी उंगलियाँ डुबोये
मेरे रक्त में
कभी उछालते
इसकी गेंद
ऊपर हवा में

कभी ये दिल
तुम्हारे हाथों में
कभी पैरों में

कभी ये मिट्टी में ठप्प
टकराये कभी
लोहे के जाल में
जा फंसे कभी
कांटे के झाड़ में

न ये दिल है
न गेंद

न ये लोंदा किसी मांस का
न गुच्छा किसी प्रकाश का

ये जो बैठी हूँ मैं
इस क्षण यहाँ

नन्ही सी ओस
चुंधियाई हुई सूर्य से

at times soaking your fingers
in my blood
at times tossing
its ball
into the air

this heart
in your hands
this heart
at your feet

Sometimes it ends up
in the dust, kicked
smashed into a steel net
caught in thorny
brambles

This is no heart
no ball

no lump of flesh
no cluster of light

As I sit here
in this moment

a speck
shining in the sun

न मैं उस हूँ
न भाप

अभी
बिल्कुल अभी

कोई ले जाएगा मुझे
तुम्हारे बादलों के पार

I am neither a dewdrop
nor vapour

now
just now

someone will take me
beyond your clouds

Afterword

When I think about Gagan Gill's work, a familiar image appears in my mind's eye. It's a Matryoshka doll: a red-shawled wooden figure, as familiar from toy shops as from folklore, unscrewed at the middle to reveal series of figurines nesting inside it. The original set of Matryoskha dolls—literally translated as "little matron"—were designed north of Moscow by Sergey Malyutin in 1890, and they depicted a mother on the outside, holding a red rooster, with her seven children inside her: five daughters, a son, and a baby. The set I picture is a later version, the one I grew up playing with, that my own mother brought with her when she came to England for the first time in the late 1980s; in this eight-doll set there are no children, just smaller and smaller exact versions of the same woman.

Gagan Gill's poems enact a genealogy of self-containment. In her frightening and lucid texts, concepts, experiences and even people are hidden within others; the future is enclosed within the present, which itself contains the past. In 'A Desire in the Bangles' the titular desire—curiously abstracted, almost personified, belonging to no one—is set inside glass bangles, which in Hindu culture are traditionally worn by a woman upon marriage and broken when she becomes a widow. Indeed, inside the girl who wears the bangles is a woman, inside whom is a 'widow to be', who is herself a container for

> that primal innocence,
> madness, death,
> whose punishment
> she will give to that man
> one day

Desire and mourning alike throb inside the glass bangles of the woman-girl-widow: grief lives inside love, and the bangles have always already been broken, even before she puts them on. Mourning, for Gill, is a state of permanence: her poetry functions partly as a record of the certainty of grief, its natural place inside all modes of life and writing. Her career-long engagement with Buddhist philosophies of impermanence centres both the constancy of sorrow and the cyclical nature of human existence in her work. These poems are lyrical distillations of individual moments in time that simultaneously extend beyond its constraints; linearity, her work leads us to understand, is just one way of reading the world.

The enmeshed relationship between death and desire has a long history of being both encoded as feminine and associated with containment. In Freud's curious 1913 essay 'The Theme of the Three Caskets', which takes its cue from *The Merchant of Venice*, which in turn borrows its plot device from the *Gesta Romanorum*, the caskets in question are, like Pandora's Box and other enclosed spaces, 'symbols of what is essential in a woman'. Women, according to Freud, contain within them the three 'inevitable relations that a man has with a woman—the woman who bears him, the woman who is his mate, and the woman who destroys him'. Like the multiple selves inside Matryoshka dolls, these 'inevitable' women are linked, too, to the three guises inhabited by the figure of the mother in the course of a man's life: 'the mother herself, the beloved one who is chosen after her pattern, and lastly the Mother Earth who receives him once more'. This idea is both an analysis of the psychic reality of a misogynist society and an entrenchment of its principles. But in Gill's poetry, this historic theme of gendered containment is rewritten—perhaps even reclaimed—through her repetitive affirmative rewriting of the canonical concept of the female body as a vessel for the cycles of time. We are born, we die, we are girls, daughters, lovers, widows, corpses, and the body of a woman contains all of those possibilities within in. Like a lyric poem itself, in which time is always doubled—the present tense of the reader and the present tense of the speaker collapse into each other each time the text is read—a woman is always inside time's passage and without it, representative of its changes and their container.

In these texts, women's desire is crucially not only a precursor to mourning but an active propulsive force of existence itself. In 'Only for a Day', the removal of a woman's attention, even if only temporary, ruptures the fabric of life irreparably. If 'she' does not think of you, 'you will vanish / in an ethereal mist', but it is not only the individual that will dissolve: 'darkness will spread to the ends of the universe'. Gill's speaker figures this destruction in ambivalently maternal language, stating that 'the umbilical cord of time / will wind round its own neck'. Who is the mother, here, and who is the child? If time itself is strangled in utero, who survives to record it? The poem, twisting away from interpretation even as it invites it, suggests that it is this 'she' who bears the responsibility for turning the source of life into an instrument of its curtailment.

Motherhood is complicated, too, by 'Child Go Home', a poem whose speaker seems to inhabit a similar space to the powerful 'she' of 'Only for a Day'. Apparently addressing a child before their conception, the biological process of fertilisation is rewritten as a philosophical dialogue that playfully subverts the question of when life can be said to begin:

> Your home is nowhere?
> Then go back to the womb
>
> No mother's womb?
> Go to father's semen.

Your father is nowhere?
Go to mum's tubes.

Is the egg there barren?

At first reading, this seems like a nursery rhyme that, riddle-like, retraces the biological process backwards in time. Yet the path the poem maps out is, at a closer reading, powerfully uncanny: the child cannot return to the 'mother's womb' because the womb does not exist. The 'father's semen' is inaccessible because the father himself is nowhere; 'mum's tubes' are populated only by barren eggs. The poem continues, absurdly and tenderly: 'Then, little one, flow away / in her menstrual blood'. The blood intermingles with desire—'just as her longing / goes down the drain– / go that way too'—and the abstract possibility of reproduction is suddenly returned to its emotional pattern, to longing and losing. The poem ends with a final address to the possible-impossible child: 'Let the girl be. / Child, go home'. The child yet-to-come is sacrificed for the life of the child-that-is; inside the girl is a mother, but she will emerge only when the time is right.

'Child Go Home' was originally published in 1989 in Gill's first collection, *Ek din lautegi larki* (*One day the girl will return*), a book in which the eponymous girl has been interpreted by critics as a symbol of the difficulties faced by predominantly middle-class urban women in a rapidly modernising India, an interpretation aided by the concomitant establishment of Delhi as a contemporary centre of urban feminist activity in the decades after Independence. The image of a pregnancy arrived unwanted and too soon, robbing a girl of her right to a childhood, is not difficult to connect with the systemic problem of sexual violence that dominates Indian society and legislature that feminist activists and human rights campaigners have been fighting to address for decades. Certainly, in Gill's work as I have read it, there is a deep commitment to social realities, including the material conditions of violence, that often manifest in the lives of women. Yet there are obvious limitations to reading these texts through a western feminist lens. In her 2012 discussion of Gill's poetry in *Bodies that Remember: Women's Indigenous Knowledge and Cosmopolitanism in South Asian Poetry*, Anita Anantharam recounts a conversation in which the poet complicated preconceived ideas of her work as explicitly or singularly feminist, declaring her work to be first and foremost a direct and sustained engagement with the teachings of Buddhism: 'I am not a feminist; you see I am a practicing Buddhist'. Gill's work is fundamentally metaphysical in its concerns; there is no singular reading of her texts.

The suffering depicted in Gill's work is abstracted suffering, the violence she invokes is abstracted violence. The tension between the need to do justice to the individual's experience of pain and the acknowledgment and acceptance of hardship as both inherent and necessary to life itself is held in a constant negotiation between the political and the spiritual content of Gill's work. The violence of her poetic imagery is a mark of her refusal to shy away from the injustice of harm, even as she reaffirms its transcendental potential. If this is a poetics of liberation, the release itself comes as much from the impersonality of cyclical human existence as it does from an engagement with mortality. Throughout these poems, an underlying concern with transfiguration and rebirth makes familiar objects strange. In 'This Water', a heart becomes 'no heart' and then 'no lump of flesh / no cluster of light'. The speaker first names what they see—colours, flowers, sunlight—and then reneges on their certainty, defining them only by negation:

at times a circle
at times a line

> is neither red
> nor white
>
> neither flower
> nor petal

Elsewhere, women are transformed into ants, bodies become dewdrops, rocks melt into nothing. The speaker of Gill's poems, in a repeated, radical act of fragmentation, imagines themselves into each of the living things they depict. The self, like the eponymous creatures of 'Fish', is defined and ultimately protected by its ability to open up its borders and boundaries: 'Into the brimming ocean / she is emptying herself incessantly / over centuries'.

In each of these texts, mourning and celebration are held in balance, as the multiplicity of each human lifetime occurs simultaneously, and the Matryoshka dolls are lined up next to each other, or, perhaps, arranged in a circle:

> You remember, don't you
> when to take a thousand forms
> when just one?
>
> ('Do You See It?')

Death is permanent only because life is, too. Gill's work, in facing up to the conditions of existence, also transfigures mourning. Just this is enough 'to turn small griefs / into vapour'.

Helen Charman

Gagan Gill is a Hindi poet, essayist and travel writer. Alongside her five critically acclaimed collections of poetry, she has published three books of essays and a much-celebrated travelogue *Awaak* (Vani Prakashan; 2009) describing a pilgrimage to Kailash Mansarovar. She has held several of India's most prominent positions in cultural journalism and was the literary editor of *Times of India* magazine *Vama* and the *Sunday Observer*. She was a visiting writer at the International Writing Program in Iowa in 1990 and the Nieman Fellow for journalism at Harvard University in 1992-93. However, after many years, she gave up her career in journalism in order to devote herself to poetry and its demands: 'the long periods of silence in her everyday life' that she considers vital to remain 'truly connected to words'.

Lucy Rosenstein graduated in Indology from Sofia University and obtained her MA and PhD in Hindi at SOAS, University of London, where she was a Lecturer for 10 years. She has published two books and numerous articles on Hindi poetry. Since 2007, the main focus of her work has been child and adolescent mental health, but she continues to be nurtured by her deep connection with poetry.

Jane Duran has published five collections of poetry with Enitharmon Press: *Breathe Now, Breathe* (1995), *Silences from the Spanish Civil War* (2002), *Coastal* (2005), *Graceline* (2010) and *American Sampler* (2014). Together with Gloria García Lorca, she translated Lorca's *Gypsy Ballads* (Enitharmon; 2011), and his *Sonnets of Dark Love* and *The Tamarit Divan* (Enitharmon; 2017).

Helen Charman is a writer and academic based in Glasgow. Her first book, *Mother State*, is forthcoming from Allen Lane. Her second pamphlet *Daddy Poem* (Spam Press; 2019) was shortlisted for the 2019 Ivan Juritz Prize; her latest, *In the Pleasure Dairy*, is published by Sad Press.

About the Poetry Translation Centre

Set up in 2004, the Poetry Translation Centre is the only UK organisation dedicated to translating, publishing and promoting contemporary poetry from Africa, Asia and Latin America. We introduce extraordinary poets from around the world to new audiences through books, online resources and bilingual events. We champion diversity and representation in the arts, and forge enduring relations with diaspora communities in the UK. We explore the craft of translation through our long-running programme of workshops which are open to all.

The Poetry Translation Centre is based in London and is an Arts Council National Portfolio organisation. To find out more about us, including how you can support our work, please visit: www.poetrytranslation.org.

About the World Poet Series

The *World Poet Series* offers an introduction to some of the world's most exciting contemporary poets in an elegant pocket-sized format. The books are presented as bilingual editions, with the English and original-language text displayed side by side. The translations themselves have emerged from specially commissioned collaborations between leading English-language poets and translators. Completing each book is an afterword essay by a UK-based poet, responding to the translations.

Gagan Gill is a Hindi poet, essayist and travel writer. Alongside her five critically acclaimed collections of poetry, she has published three books of essays and a much-celebrated travelogue *Awaak* (Vani Prakashan; 2009) describing a pilgrimage to Kailash Mansarovar. She has held several of India's most prominent positions in cultural journalism and was the literary editor of *Times of India* magazine *Vama* and the *Sunday Observer*. She was a visiting writer at the International Writing Program in Iowa in 1990 and the Nieman Fellow for journalism at Harvard University in 1992-93. However, after many years, she gave up her career in journalism in order to devote herself to poetry and its demands: 'the long periods of silence in her everyday life' that she considers vital to remain 'truly connected to words'.